I0122670

The Bible Cure For Anxiety

Ancient Answers For Stress Management And Anxiety Relief

HENRY MATLOCK

ISBN 978-0615788388

Praise for *The Bible Cure For Anxiety*

"Although these are ancient answers we need to be reminded daily of our part in living without anxiety. Henry reminds us that our prayers don't change God – they change us. Be encouraged that regardless of circumstances we can use these principles to live as examples of gratitude, hope and peace."

- Dan Miller, life coach and author *48 Days to the Work You Love*

ॐ ॐ

"It's easy to let the worries of this world consume our thoughts. Henry uses Scripture to bring us back to the truths that offer deep abiding peace."

- Erin K. Casey, Contributing Editor, *SUCCESS Magazine* and author of the *Zany Zia's Hats to Where Adventure Series*

ॐ ॐ

Praise for *The Bible Cure For Anxiety*

"In a concise and simple manner, Henry Matlock brings the first century words of the apostle Paul into the 21st century, explaining how the process of prayer and meditation can ultimately achieve peace in today's hurried and stress-filled world. Short, not preachy, Henry shows how these words are as relevant today as they were almost two thousand years ago."

- Louise Reichert, author of *The Prisoner's Prayer Book*

൭ ൲

"When anxiety sets in, the voices around us provide many solutions. But there is only one voice that should be speaking louder. This book has that voice."

- Paul Mayende, author of *Into the City Church*

൭ ൲

Praise for *The Bible Cure For Anxiety*

"In our anxiety-filled world, it's easy to say that we shouldn't be anxious; but that's much easier said than done. In *The Bible Cure for Anxiety*, Henry Matlock takes readers from just knowing what they should do, to actually implementing biblically-rooted principles in order to accomplish it. Walking through Philippians 4:5-9, Henry draws out the key truths of depending on God and using the guidelines laid out in the Bible. These truths will help you to truly move from a life of anxiety to the peace of God. If you're looking for relief from worry and disquiet, *The Bible Cure for Anxiety* is an excellent resource to help you find God's answer to your struggle."

- Randy Crane, Life & Personal Development Coach, Leaving Conformity Coaching

ഔ ൙

Praise for *The Bible Cure For Anxiety*

"*The Bible Cure for Anxiety* is a lovely healing balm for those who are facing anxiety in their lives. Being that an astounding 18% of our population is affected by anxiety, my hope is that those who suffer from this take time out for their soul to soak up the wisdom and reminders of what God wants for us within these pages. Henry's book pulls out intentional action steps from His word and puts it in easy to understand teachings that will help you find peace and contentment. Love the powerful underlying reminder message that God ultimately controls all situations we face in life."

- Jen McDonough, Motivational Storyteller and author of *Living Beyond Awesome* and *Living Beyond Rich*

෨ ෬

Praise for *The Bible Cure For Anxiety*

"*The Bible Cure For Anxiety* is a practical guide to relieving the fear of stress and anxiety felt by many of us in today's world. Henry not only encourages us to make the decision to be free of anxiety but also introduces us to the power and the tools needed to do so. If you are experiencing stress or anxiety, be free. Henry Matlock's *The Bible Cure For Anxiety* is a must read."

- Veronica Sutherland, author of *Marriage Is A Conversation* and *Wisdom of Ole Time Jamaican People*

Dedication

To the memory of Jeannie G. Matlock. Thank you for your example of love and peace. I look forward to seeing you again.

Table of Contents

Preface

With the harsh reality of all that is going on in the world around us - high unemployment, foreclosure, disease, murder, rape, identity theft, addiction, suicide, internet scams, home invasions - it is easy to understand people being in an almost constant state of anxiety. Because of these and other causes, anxiety disorders are the most common mental illness in the United States, affecting 40 million adults in the United States age 18 and older (18% of the U.S. population).

On the night that He was betrayed, shortly after Jesus told the disciples that they were unable to follow where He was going, He comforted them with these words:

> *"Peace I leave with you; my peace I give you.... Do not let your hearts be troubled and do not be afraid." John 14:27*

But ***how*** do we fend off trouble from our hearts when there is impending trouble looming all around us?

The Bible invites followers of Christ to cast all our anxiety on Him because he cares for us. (See 1 Peter 5:7) But Peter does not offer a method for casting our cares.

Many of us know ***that*** we are supposed to keep our hearts from being troubled, and ***that*** we are supposed to not be afraid, and ***that*** we are supposed to cast our anxiety on God. But what most people do not know is ***how*** - that is, the method to complying with these divinely-inspired instructions. This book strives to answer this question to help you, the reader, live a life free from anxiety and undue stress.

Acknowledgments

My beautiful bride, Johnnie, you are everything I ever wanted, and everything I didn't realize I needed, in a wife. Thank you for lifting me up, for keeping me grounded, and for sharing this wonderful journey with me.

Dad, Greg, Roz and Brian, you have my heartfelt appreciation for your love and support that come without conditions. I am truly grateful for each of you.

Thanks to the members of the 48Days.net community, Dan, Joanne, Kent, Erin, Jen, Kimanzi, Scott, and a host of others for your leadership, your example, your wisdom, and your encouragement. You mean more to me than you know. You all are amazing, and I am honored to be a part of such a special group of people.

Introduction

Henry Matlock has, once again, written a practical and inspiring book, *The Bible Cure for Anxiety*. I have known Henry for a few years, and I've personally witnessed his philosophy for greatness---serving others. His beautiful words of encouragement and instruction have uplifted many a downhearted soul.

So often, our minds are burdened with stress and anxiety over the following areas:

-our health
-our job security
-our financial state
-our relationships
-our self-worth

Except for a few medical conditions, much of our anxiety is self-imposed. We tend to focus our minds on the worst-case outcome rather than trusting in the Knower of all outcomes.

With a passion for God and people's spiritual and physical wellbeing, Henry, through his book, reminds us that God gives us the ability to conquer anxiety. He shows us, through God's glorious scripture, how we can overcome this relentless tormentor.

Henry skillfully unlocks the meaning to key passages in the fourth chapter of the Book of Philippians. These scriptures help draw us into the very presence of God and filter our minds from the destructive crud of the world. So take a minute and change the filter. Listen to Henry's words. The engines of your thought life will run smoother, and your soul will enjoy a consistent, lasting peace.

S. Scott Johnson
Author and Blogger
www.sscottjohnson.wordpress.com

Foreword

Anxiety (definition) - A feeling of worry, nervousness, or unease, typically about an imminent event or something with an uncertain outcome.

According to the National Institute of Mental Health, anxiety is a normal coping reaction to stress. It helps the employee deal with a tense situation in the workplace, the student study harder for an exam, and the presenter keep focused on an important speech.

However, if rather than relatively light and infrequent episodes of anxiety, one experiences an excessive, irrational dread of everyday situations, it can make life very difficult.

Generalized anxiety (GA) can manifest in a number of ways, such as a constant worry of things big or small, difficulty concentrating, or moodiness. There can even be physical symptoms including headaches or other aches and pains that have physical cause, sweating, hot flashes, and a feeling like you need to throw up when you are worried.

Modern society's answer to people who experience GA is to offer some combination of medication and/or psychotherapy, or "talk therapy", as treatment options. According to Margaret Wehrenberg, Psy.D., a licensed psychologist, medication is considered by insurance and drug companies to be the primary treatment option for anxiety. However, the excessive use of medication "is losing public favor as people realize that they have unpleasant side effects and their symptoms reemerge when they stop using the drugs."[1]

---

[1] Source: *The 10 Best-Ever Anxiety Management Techniques: Understanding How Your Brain Makes You Anxious and What You Can Do to Change It*

The Bible Cure For Anxiety offers a Bible based response and an alternative option for anxiety sufferers.

Chapter One: Prayer

The Lord is near. *6Do not be anxious about anything, but in everything, by prayer and petition, with thanksgiving, present your requests to God. 7And the peace of God, which transcends all understanding, will guard your hearts and your minds in Christ Jesus.*

- Philippians 4:5b-7

What causes you to be anxious? Is it financial distress? Is it strife in relationships? Is it loneliness? Is it having more responsibilities than you can handle? Is it wanting greater responsibilities than those with which you've been entrusted?

Or maybe it's starting a new chapter in your life like going to school, having a baby, moving, starting a new career or business venture, retirement, facing a significant health challenge, joining with another in holy matrimony, or saying good-bye to something or someone that you care (or once cared) a great deal about.

All of these circumstances share at least two things in common, albeit in varying degrees. The first of these commonalities is that the outcomes or resolutions are unknown. When you look at what you know for certain about your situation and what you would like to know about it, you can see there is a significant knowledge gap.

The second shared characteristic is that the outcomes or resolutions are out of your control. Sure, with moving, for instance, you can plan the actual move. In fact, you may have decided upon the address, the moving date, and whether to hire a moving service or to do it yourself. But what you can't control are such things as the type of neighbors you will have or the extent to which you may miss the unique qualities of your current residence that helped make it a home.

The good news is that the answer to both of these common traits is found in the same place. God knows the resolutions, and God has ultimate control over every situation you will ever face. And the Bible provides us with instructions to help us take full advantage of these basic truths.

Decide

If, in fact, you desire not to suffer from anxiety, then the first thing you have to do is decide that you will not be an anxiety sufferer. The single most powerful moment in a person's life is the instant in which she makes a decision.

From Philippians 4:6: "*Do not be anxious about anything....*" Notice what the writer of this text, Paul, is *not* saying here. He does not say, "I sure hope your anxiety subsides some day," or "I pray the Lord purges you of the spirit of anxiety." Clearly, Paul is issuing a charge to the readers of this letter. The message he is conveying is that we have been graced with the ability and the freedom to choose whether to live with anxiety or to live anxiety free. We can decide whether to allow the way things may look or feel at the moment to determine our mental state, or to trust that the situation will work together for our good because of our kinship with the Divine.

Reverence

Aside from having a medical disorder, the only way we experience anxiety is by having a distorted perception of the situations that we face. From that perception, we exaggerate the likelihood and/or the results of having an undesired outcome. As a consequence, we experience an exaggerated level of fear that we'll suffer the undesired outcome. How you perceive your circumstances will determine how you handle them mentally and emotionally.

That said, put your situations in proper perspective. I encourage you to perceive God's presence with you. Paul says in verse 5 that the Lord is *near*. The Almighty God - who loves you, and who is so much greater than every situation you will ever face - is right there with you while you are facing your challenges.

Paul instructs the readers to pray. "Prayer" as used in verse 6 refers to a general prayer of worship. You are paying God reverent honor and homage for his goodness, his mercy, his grace and for his all-encompassing love.

Petition

While you are praying with reverence for God, you are also to incorporate petition into your prayer. This is a different kind of prayer. A petition is a prayer for particular benefits.

While some people may believe that this is self centered or "carnal" praying, there is biblical support for praying specifically for something good from God. In James' letter to the twelve tribes of Israel, he wrote:

> *"You do not have, because you do not ask God." James 4:2*

Jesus Himself instructed His followers:

> *"Ask and it will be given to you...." Matthew 7:7*

And He explains how it is within the Father's character to grant your request:

> *"If you...though you are evil, know how to give good gifts to your children, how much more will your Father in heaven give good gifts to those who ask him!" Matthew 7:11*

It is important to keep in mind that your prayers of petition be based on right motives. Immediately after James wrote, "You do not have, because you do not ask God," he penned this weighty statement:

> *"When you ask, you do not receive, because you ask **with wrong motives**, that you may spend what you get on your pleasures." James 4:3 (emphasis added)*

Fortunately, James also provides the key to ensuring that your requests align with God's desire for you:

> *"Submit yourselves, then, to God." James 4:7a*

By submitting to God, your focus shifts from you to him and his purpose, plan and desire for you. Your desire is to please God, and your aim is to satisfy God rather than to satisfy yourself.

Gratitude

Let's take another look at Philippians 4:6: "*Do not be anxious about anything, but in everything, **by prayer and petition, with thanksgiving**, present your requests to God*." Notice that the bolded portion does not read, "by prayer, petition and thanksgiving." If it read that way, then that would indicate that we should add a prayer of gratitude to our prayer of reverence and prayer of petition. When you offer your prayer of reverence and petition, you are to do so **with** thanksgiving. In other words, to receive relief from anxiety, thanksgiving is the manner in which we are to offer our prayer of reverence and petition.

So while paying God reverent honor and homage, you are doing so with a heart of gratitude. And your words may follow suit:

> "Thank you, Lord, for your faithfulness, mercy and grace. And thank you for loving me and for never leaving nor forsaking me."[2]

Likewise, while you are asking God to meet specific requests, you are to do so with gratitude. For example, if you are anxious because you have been asked for the first time to lead a major project:

> "Lord, thank you for gracing me with wisdom, guidance

---

[2] These prayers are provided for illustrative purposes only. I believe that prayer is an intimate and personal spiritual discipline. In this light, my aim here is to guide the reader in prayer, rather than to provide specific words to pray.

and direction to fulfill my
duties well; and thank you
for the project's successful
completion."[2]

So rather than praying *for* the desired
outcome, you are praying *from* the
desired outcome. The day after Jesus had
cursed the fig tree and Peter drew His
attention to its being withered from the
roots, in his reply Jesus told him:

> *"Whatever things you ask
> for in prayer, believe that
> you **have received** it, and it
> will be yours." Mark 11:24
> (emphasis added)*

You do not believe that you *will* receive it.
Instead, you believe that your request *has
already been granted*. When you have
already received something that you have
wanted and requested, you don't keep
asking for it. Instead, your immediate
reaction is one of joy for having your
desire fulfilled, and gratitude to the One
who fulfilled it.

I remember waking up one Christmas morning when I was a boy seeing my first bicycle beside the tree. I was elated to have the bike and grateful to a certain jolly old elf for bringing it to me. Why should we react any differently when God *has fulfilled* our requests?

If you are confident and know that God has granted what it is that you just prayed for, then gratitude is the immediate, appropriate and natural response of the believer.

The Result of Prayer

The Bible promises that peace will result from your prayer of reverence and petition, with thanksgiving:

> *And the peace of God, which transcends all understanding, will guard your hearts and your minds in Christ Jesus. Philippians 4:7*

The word for peace describes the harmonized relationships between God and man, accomplished through the gospel and the *sense of rest and contentment* consequent thereon. Paul wrote that this sense of rest and contentment will guard your heart[3] and your mind by keeping watch out in advance to defend them from the enemy force which, as referenced in this passage, is anxiety.[4]

It is helpful to note that this peace keeps watch for anxiety *in advance*. The earlier you pray, the earlier you are dispatching peace to its guard post. The earlier that peace is posted, the sooner it can spot anxiety's attempts to advance and the sooner it can sufficiently defend your mind.

---

[3] "Heart" refers to the spirit of a man or "the hidden man" as discussed in I Peter 3:4.

[4] The word for "guard" means to be a watcher in advance, i.e. to mount guard as a sentinel; figuratively, to hem in or protect. It is a military term meaning to keep by guarding. In this scripture, it is used of the sense of the Christian's security when he puts all his matters into the hand of God. It can also mean a benevolent custody and watchful guardianship.

Chapter Two: Meditation

Finally, brothers, whatever is true, whatever is noble, whatever is right, whatever is pure, whatever is lovely, whatever is admirable - if anything is excellent or praiseworthy - think about such things.

- Philippians 4:8

The mind is an amazing thing. It has been said that where the mind goes, the man will follow. I have found this to be true in my life. For example, when I spend my quiet time recalling the way in which I have interacted with others, and thinking about how I may behave, say, more patiently in the future, I find that in my next interactions I exercise more patience.

Likewise, I find it easy to be more effective and productive in a certain area of responsibility after I have spent time beforehand thinking about doing so. There have been several occasions when I could actually sense my efforts being guided by a wisdom I had not acquired through life experience. Conversely, if I am attempting to lose weight and to eat healthier and I think about pepperoni pizza throughout the day, that is when I am most likely to "take a day off" from my eating plan.

Nowadays we have so many things competing for our attention. It can be a challenge to stay focused on what is important. Even when we are careful to filter the media that we view, listen to or read, undesired and counterproductive messages can still get past our defenses. So we have to be intentional in focusing our thought lives toward the direction in which we want to head. This need to be intentional is especially true if that direction is to live free from the anxiety that this world oftentimes seems to promote.

The psychological community recognizes that "people have great power to use their brains to change their brains."[5] Paul instructed the readers of his letter to be intentional on thinking about things that fall under certain specific categories. Let's take a closer look at each one.

Whatever Is True

This is the first category Paul encouraged the readers to meditate on. The word for true means primarily "unconcealed, manifest." To be clear, he was not saying that we should meditate on the unconcealed or manifest thing that may spark anxiety. Instead, Paul was saying that we should think about the things that have been revealed to us and manifested in our lives by God. God has revealed and manifested his goodness toward you in a multitude of ways. Remember them. God's love for you has not changed. So remain rooted in the truths that God is

[5] Source: *The 10 Best-Ever Anxiety Management Techniques: Understanding How Your Brain Makes You Anxious and What You Can Do to Change It*

the same yesterday, today and forever, and that his love for you never waivers.

Whatever Is Noble

This is the second category of things Paul instructed the readers to ponder on. The word for noble denotes that which inspires reverence and awe. For me, that which is most reverent and awe-inspiring is the love of God toward each of us. In light of mankind's sinful state and our subsequent inability to fulfill the law, and because of God's abounding love for us, he sent us his only Son from heaven. Because of Jesus' love for us, although He lived free from sin, He paid the price for all sin by freely enduring the suffering and shame of a slow and public execution.

Consequently, I get to spend eternity with Him. And what's more, because God has established me in his love, I can "*grasp how wide and long and high and deep is the love of Christ*" and I "*may be filled to the measure of all the fullness of God.*" (see Ephesians 3:16-19) How amazing is that! Think about it.

"Noble" also points to seriousness of purpose. God has uniquely gifted and equipped you to fulfill a unique purpose. There is a specific service that you are to provide while on this earth. Ponder that. If you have never thought about the truth that you have a purpose for being here, then it behooves you to take some time and to meditate on it.

Put whatever you find yourself anxious about up against your divine purpose to see how it measures up. Ask yourself, "What is the correlation between what I am anxious about and God's purpose for me?" For instance, say that your divine purpose is to share a message that either helps or gives hope and inspiration to others; yet you experience anxiety when you speak in front of an audience. Even if you would prefer to share your message either through writing or by sharing it in a one-on-one setting, I would say there is a direct correlation.

Here's why: fulfilling your purpose, i.e. sharing the message, is the primary objective. The medium or media you use (e.g. blogging, writing books, individual coaching, or public speaking) is merely a conduit through which you fulfill your purpose. The method is of secondary importance. Just like a dog is not wagged by its tail, the secondary thing is not meant to control the primary thing.

The purpose of sharing the message trumps the method by which you accomplish this goal. There are people who need to benefit from the service you provide who, in this example, may never read your blog or book and whom you may never meet one-on-one. However, if you include public speaking among the methods by which you share your message, then that will make the message available to those people who might hear you at a live event or watch you on a DVD or on YouTube.

Meditate on your unique purpose and how it can benefit others, and compare it to any fears or insecurities you may have. Your contemplation will give you a much better perspective on how both the purpose and the anxiety measure in the grand scheme of things.

The word for noble also refers to self-respect in conduct. Some anxieties result from doing things we are not meant to do. Some other anxieties emerge from failing to do things we should be doing. Examples of ways by which you can exhibit self-respect include communicating sincerely, not indulging in much wine, and not pursuing dishonest gain (see I Timothy 3:8), as well as refraining from malicious talk, being temperate, being trustworthy in everything (see I Timothy 3:11), being self-controlled, and being sound in faith, in love and in endurance (see Titus 2:2).

When you conduct yourself with self-respect, then that behavior elicits the respect of others who observe you. That respect of the observers will strengthen your witness and, ultimately, will redirect their attention and respect to God. So think about the ways you conduct yourself, both while you are alone and while you are interacting with others.

Whatever Is Right

This is the third category of things Paul wanted the readers to meditate about. The word for right (also translated "just") means equitable in character or act; by implication, the definition also extends to mean innocent or holy. Unfortunately, whether in the courts, in government or in business, stories of injustice and corruption abound. Expending a significant amount of thought about such things is bound to bring on anxiety at some point.

Fortunately, the Bible shares some things that are right and just that we should bear in mind. Jesus said that His judgment is just (John 5:30). We who obey the law of faith are declared right (see Romans 2:13, 3:10, 3:20 and 3:27). The ultimate punishment for every violation and disobedience of those who are not heirs of God's salvation is just (see Hebrews

2:2-3). The ways of the Lord are just (see Revelation 15:3).

Despite the unjust things we may hear and read about, there are also things in our world that are right and just. Spend some time pondering those.

Whatever Is Pure

This is the fourth category of things Paul instructed the readers to contemplate. The word for pure signifies being pure from every fault. Without exception, every instance of this word being used in the Bible is not with respect to inanimate objects such as precious metals.

The word is used with respect to people - specifically with respect to followers of Christ. One example includes Paul's instruction to Timothy to keep himself pure (I Timothy 5:22). So we are to think about how we can live without fault.

The word for pure also is given as a quality of the "wisdom that comes from heaven" in contrast to the "wisdom" (i.e. envy and selfish ambition) that is earthly, unspiritual, of the devil (see James 3:13-18). Meditate on how godly wisdom can permeate those areas of your life in which you find yourself envious of others or in which you have ambitions where you stand to benefit more than others.

In I John 3:3, this word is used to describe God himself: "Everyone who has this help in him purifies himself, just as he (God) is pure." The passage goes on to say that "in him is no sin" (see John 3:4). So ponder God's purity. Realize that your born-again spirit has recaptured the image and likeness of the perfectly pure God, and that you can live purely as a result.

Whatever Is Lovely

This is the fifth category of things Paul instructed the readers to ponder on. This word for lovely is presumed to be rooted in the word phileo (love), which means to have affection for, denoting a personal attachment. Phileo should be distinguished against agapao (love). The distinction between the two verbs finds a

conspicuous instance in the narrative of
John 21:15-17:

> **99** *When they had finished eating,*
> *Jesus said to Simon Peter,*
> *'Simon son of John, do you*
> *truly (agapao) love me more than*
> *these?' 'Yes, Lord,' he said 'you*
> *know that I (phileo) love you.' Jesus*
> *said, 'Feed my lambs.'*
>
> *16 Again Jesus said, 'Simon son of*
> *John, do you truly (agapao) love*
> *me?' He answered, 'Yes, Lord, you*
> *know that I (phileo) love you.' Jesus*
> *said, 'Take care of my sheep.'*
>
> *17 The third time he said to him,*
> *'Simon son of John, do you (phileo)*
> *love me?' Peter was hurt because*
> *Jesus asked him the third time, 'Do*
> *you (phileo) love me?' He said,*
> *'Lord, you know all things; you*
> *know that I (phileo) love you.' Jesus*
> *said, 'Feed my sheep.'"*

The context itself indicates that agapao in
the first two questions suggests the "love"

that values and esteems. It is an unselfish "love," ready to serve. The use of phileo in Peter's answers and the Lord's third question, conveys the thought of **cherishing the Object above all else**, of manifesting an **affection characterized by constancy**, from the motive of the **highest reverence**.[6]

Some anxieties can arise from misplaced affections. Loving things that are unable to love you in return, e.g. money, fame, power or careers, ultimately does not satisfy. And being in unhealthy relationships can cause undue levels of stress and angst. So meditate on whatever it is that you cherish above all else. My hope is that the primary Object of your affection is God. If it is not, meditate of why that is the case. If God is the primary recipient of your affections, meditate on whether, and to what degree, constancy is manifested toward the Object of your affection, as well as the

---

[6] Source: *The New Strong's Expanded Exhaustive Concordance of the Bible*, Red Letter Edition, 2001

underlying motives of your affection toward him.

Whatever Is Admirable

This is the sixth category of things Paul instructed the readers to ponder on. This word for admirable is a combination of two other words: "good" and "saying", i.e. rumor or fame. The first word means "good" in the sense of profit or advantage: worth; benefit. Jesus used "good" in this sense when he told His disciples, "For you have the poor with you always, and whenever you wish you may do them **good**: but Me you do not have always." (Mark 14:7 NKJV)

The second word is used to describe the fame throughout the land of Jesus raising a little girl from the dead (see Mark 9:26), as well as the fame throughout Galilee of Jesus' ministry there (see Luke 4:14). So combining the meaning of these two words, this one word for admirable means having word spread about and being known for providing advantage or benefit to others.

Is this the kind of reputation you have within your community? Does your circle of friends, family, coworkers, classmates, or fellow church members know you as someone who gives and serves for the benefit of other people? Think about Jesus' fame for doing good, and what it required of Him to earn it. And think about the reputation you have earned up to now, and what you can do better, differently, more of, or less of in order to earn a reputation that is more like that of Jesus.

Excellent And Praiseworthy

While the six categories discussed previously are specific types of things you should ponder on, excellence and praiseworthiness are broad qualities that you should use as filters for your thought life. If something is excellent, it possesses outstanding quality or superior merit; it is remarkably good. If something is praiseworthy, it deserves approval or admiration, or it deserves grateful homage in words or song.

I am sure you would consider things that are true, noble, right, pure, lovely, and admirable as being excellent and praiseworthy. That is why it benefits you to think about things that fit into these categories. If something does not pass through the filters of excellence and praiseworthiness, do yourself a favor and avoid mulling over it.

Chapter Three: Put Into Practice

[I]f there be any virtue, and if there be any praise, think on these things. [9]Those things, which ye have both learned, and received, and heard, and seen in me, do: and the God of peace shall be with you.

- Philippians 4:8b-9 KJV

The six categories of things Paul wrote to meditate about (things that are true, noble, right, pure, lovely and admirable) would all be considered as godly qualities. As such, not only are they worthy of meditation, but they are also worthy of practice and emulation.

Immediately after Paul counseled the readers to think on things that make it through the filters of excellence and praiseworthiness, he instructed them to put into practice **those things** that they had learned and received and heard from him, as well as **those things** that they had witnessed in him. Given the proximity of these statements to each other, I believe Paul was not referring to two sets of things - one set to think about and another set to practice. Instead, I believe he was referring to the same set of things to both meditate on and to put into practice.

As stated in the previous chapter, we can experience some anxieties from failing to do things we should be doing. This can be a more subtle form of anxiety. It can be like "a splinter in your mind."[7] It can be more of a constant, nagging source of discomfort in your soul that can only be eased by removal.

While you are meditating on the things that are excellent and praiseworthy, do not be surprised if you perceive a prompting to take some action that aligns

[7] Quote from *The Matrix*®

with one or more of the six categories. In fact, here is a bold prediction: if you spend time meditating on things within these six categories, you can expect to be prompted to modify your behavior in some way that will reflect at least one of them.

It would be wise to have a pen and either a pad or a journal handy while you are meditating, so you can write down the actions God prompts you to take. It is amazing how we can forget even the most vivid and profound of thoughts and realizations over time. If we record them right away, we can always go back and refer to them.

Then go ahead and take the necessary steps to do what you have been prompted to do. Pray for the wisdom, courage, direction and anything else you will need in order to follow through on the action in a way that pleases God.

The Result of Meditation and Practice

Do not allow thoughts of what could happen when you change your behavior make you anxious. On the contrary, Paul provides us with a comforting promise to those who both meditate on and practice excellent and praiseworthy behavior.

> *And the God of peace will be with you. Philippians 4:9b*

Recall that this word for peace describes *the sense of rest and contentment* consequent to the harmonized relationships between God and man, which was accomplished through the gospel. The God who is the source of this sense of rest and contentment is present with you. As the psalmist wrote, "In Your presence is **fullness of joy**...." (Psalm 16:11b NKJV, emphasis added) And where there is fullness of anything, there is no room for anything else - including anxiety.

Put Into Practice

Conclusion: Walk In(to) Peace

You do not have to live with anxiety. The Bible makes that clear; and it even provides us with the tools we need to conquer anxiety. The beginning and the end of the scriptural passage we covered informs us that the presence of God opens the door to the peace that is available to every believer.

> *The Lord is near. Philippians 4:5b*

> *And the God of peace will be with you. Philippians 4:9b*

And while God's presence opens the door, it is up to each of us to walk through it. Hear the words of the prophet Isaiah:

> *Thou wilt keep him in perfect peace, whose mind is stayed on thee: **because he trusteth in thee**. Isaiah 26:3 KJV (emphasis added)*

Ultimately, having trust in God is the only way to having a life of peace. Even when you face things that can stir up anxiety, your trust in God can give you peace that boggles the mind (see Philippians 4:7).

So rather than following the steps provided in this book in a mechanical or legalistic manner, I invite you to follow the steps with a heart that trusts God. You can trust God because he loves you (see John 3:16), he has plans for you to prosper you and not to harm you, and he has plans to give you hope and a future (see Jeremiah 29:11), and he will not leave you or forsake you (see Deuteronomy 31:6).

When you pray, trust God to hear and answer your prayers. When you meditate, trust God to guide and direct your thoughts. When you take action, trust God to bless your efforts.

God is with you. Walk in(to) peace.

Bonus Chapter: First Things Last

One may presume that this book is written solely for Christians. That is not the case. People from all walks of life suffer from anxiety, and I wanted to provide a resource to help them. However, nothing I wrote about applies or even really matters if you haven't received Jesus Christ as your Lord and Savior.

If you desire to have true peace, not just here on earth, but for all eternity, pray a sincere prayer, expressing the sentiments below:

> *Lord Jesus Christ, I believe You died and rose from the grave to purchase a place in Heaven for me. Lord Jesus, come into my life, take control of my life; forgive my sins and save me. I repent of my sins and now place my trust in You for my salvation. I accept this free gift of eternal life.*

The Bible says, "For with the heart man believes unto righteousness; and with the mouth confession is made unto salvation. For whosoever shall call upon the name of the Lord shall be saved." (Romans 10:10, 13).

Welcome to the family.

Additional Resources

Here are some other resources that cover the topic of stress and anxiety from a biblical perspective.

Fake Fear: A Biblical Guide to Dealing with Stress, Worry and Anxiety by Matthew Noble

Prayer to Relieving Stress and Anxiety by Sister Mary

Anxiety Attacked by John F. MacArthur, Jr.

Illuminating The Darkness: A Fresh and Effective Solution to Depression, Stress, and Anxiety by Noel Dear

Biblical Solutions to Anxiety, Depression, Fear, Worry and Obsessive Thinking by Steve Leavitt and Tommy Nelson

Worry ~ The Bible Speaks by Leroy Freeman

Scripture Relief: Anxiety and Fear by Andrew O'Donnell

Anxious for Nothing: God's Cure for the Cares of Your Soul by John MacArthur

About The Author

Henry Matlock is an ordained Christian preacher, who is thoroughly convinced that there is hope and help for people in all walks of life that can be found only as a result of establishing and building a personal and intimate relationship with the living God. Henry believes that prayer, meditation, worship, praise, and especially study of the Bible unlock doors to successful living that are otherwise inaccessible to us.

A native Arkansan, Henry graduated from the Sam M. Walton College of Business at the University of Arkansas with an undergraduate degree in Finance. Henry also has earned graduate degrees in Business Administration, Finance, and Health Administration.

Having worked in healthcare administration for more than 10 years, Henry is board certified in healthcare management and is a Fellow of the American College of Healthcare Executives, the world's premier association of leaders in the field of healthcare administration. He also serves his local community in various capacities.

Daily Deposits for the Soul, Henry's first book, became an Amazon bestseller in its category in the United States, the United Kingdom, and Germany.

Henry is blessed to be happily married to his best friend and sweetheart of many years. He and Johnnie strive to model Christ and Church every day and to demonstrate before the world the beauty and joy of marriage.

You can follow Henry on his personal blog, henrymatlock.com, where he writes on faith, conveying your message, entrepreneurship, and wellness. You can also follow Henry on Twitter, @henrymatlock, and you can email Henry at henry@henrymatlock.com.